The Essential Guide to Puberty in Girls

How to Talk to Your Daughter about Sex, Puberty, and a Girl's First Period

by Stacy Billows

Table of Contents

Introduction

If it were only up to parents, every mom and dad would want their darling daughter to remain a little girl forever. Sadly, all parents need to face the fact that their one day, their adorable chubby-cheek princess will grow up to be a young lady. When your daughter starts to face the changes and challenges that come along with puberty – the most trying point of her young life so far – she will need you to be there to guide her.

Puberty marks your daughter's physical and emotional transition from a child into a young woman. This time can be confusing for a 13-year old, a 12-year old, and especially for a 10 or 11-year old early bloomer. This is why it's important for every parent to prepare their child for the changes ahead on the horizon. When your daughter knows what's coming and she can understand why these changes are happening, then she will be better prepared to handle puberty. If a young girl is educated about the physical as well as the emotional effects brought on by adolescence, then her chances of turning into a well-adjusted young lady with minimal drama are much improved.

This book is a guide for every parent out there who's blessed with a daughter. Now that your little girl isn't so little anymore, you will need to help her as she journeys into the next phase of her life. So equip yourself here with all the guidance you'll need on how to talk to her about puberty, her first period, and sex. It's important to be prepared with what to say, when to say, and how to say it. This book will help to prepare you as you take on one of the most important duties of a parent. Let's get started!

Chapter 1: A Parent's Responsibility

If you've seen the 1976, Brian De Palma, horror film, "Carrie", you'll understand why it's important to prepare your daughter for puberty. In the movie, Carrie, played by Sissy Spacek, had her first period in the school shower, right after gym class. The poor girl didn't know what was happening, and thinking that she must be injured, she ran to her classmates for help. Unfortunately, kids can be cruel and so they laughed at her and threw tampons and pads at her face. Movies tend to exaggerate but this excerpt reminds us to be prepared. As parents to a daughter, it is your responsibility to teach your child about puberty, menstruation, and sex. And yes, while it is true that many schools include sex education in their high school curriculum, this topic is best explained by a loving and caring parent.

Why Parents Need to Take an Active Role

In the movie, "Carrie", the mother, played by Piper Laurie, was a mentally unstable religious fanatic. She believed that sex and anything related to it were sins. She, therefore, did not educate her teenage daughter about puberty and sex. As a result, her daughter had to find out about menstruation the hard, embarrassing way. Again, the movies have artistic license to exaggerate. In real life, we will not intentionally keep our daughter in the dark about something she needs to be prepared to face.

And yet, there are still many parents who neglect to take an active role when it comes to educating their child about puberty and sex. Here are the more common reasons that parents give:

Excuse #1: She'll learn all about that from sex education class.

Some parents think that they don't have to talk to their kids about puberty or sex because the school will do it for them. It is likely that they themselves were taught the basics by their own school teachers. But what parents should understand is the school is only there to supplement learning. It is the primary duty of parents to prepare their child for the major stages in their lives.

Also, no matter how well prepared and comprehensive the Sex Ed class is designed, pubescent children may not fully absorb the weighty information they are presented with. A classroom full of teasing teenagers is also not the best place to clarify and bring up questions that your daughter might have. Teachers are equipped to provide a mechanical or detailed narrative of how things work and where things go, but it can leave the student feeling detached from the whole topic. Your family values and personal expectations may differ significantly from that of the educator's. As a parent guiding your daughter in her journey, your words offer a reassuring personal touch – something that the child will connect with. A parent can tailor the tone of the conversation to make it just right for her mental and emotional maturity, as opposed to a generic classroom lecture meant for a group. The daughter will feel more comfortable to ask questions. Most importantly, she trusts her parents and so she will be able to absorb the information more readily and own its corresponding responsibilities more wholeheartedly.

Excuse #2: It's taboo to talk about it.

Even in these modern times, there are still parents who consider sex and other related topics as taboo. In an environment where sex is treated like a secret and is a prohibited topic of conversation, the child will learn to ask her questions somewhere else. She will covertly seek answers on her own – from other people (maybe from wiser, worldly friends) and other sources (books, magazines and the internet) which are not always accurate or age-appropriate.

Modern-minded parents, today, are more flexible when it comes to discussing sex with their kids. They understand the importance of doing so and the need to teach their kids early about it. These parents know that if they don't tell their kids what they need to know now, they will get the information from other potentially unreliable and harmful sources.

Excuse # 3: I just wouldn't know what to say.

In reality, many parents postpone or skip "The Talk" with their teenagers because they don't really know how to broach the subject of sex to their kids. They may not know how to explain why women have bigger breasts than men, how and why women need to menstruate, why they feel sexually aroused, and whether or not it's okay to touch themselves. Aside from lack of knowledge, parents can feel embarrassed and uncomfortable discussing these topics with their child. The best advice for parents is to prepare their own scripts and be armed with as many answers to potential questions as possible so that they are more confident and less embarrassed in discussing puberty and sex with their daughter. With adequate preparation, parents can introduce the topic, explain in detail, and accurately answer all the questions that could be confusing the child.

Excuse # 4: I'm busy.

"I have no time to do it" is probably the worst excuse a parent can use to get out of this duty but amazingly, many still use it. Because of their busy schedules, parents will delay or even skip giving the sex talk to their children. However, if you are a parent with a hectic timetable, just think about how many minutes you'd actually spend when you have this sit-down with your daughter. It should only be around 30 minutes to an hour at most. That one hour talk with you can be all that she needs to deal with the pressures of the adolescent stage. Stop being busy for a minute, and block off time to have "the talk" with your girl. She needs your help and guidance.

Excuse # 5: I'll explain when she asks.

Among the biggest mistakes of parents is waiting until their child asks about the changes happening to her body, their feelings, and sex. You have to consider that your child may never ask. In this case, will you think that she does not need any answers? A number of parents maintain the wrong belief that if their daughter does not ask, then she does not want to know. Even if this were true, it does not change the fact that moms and dads need to have "the talk" with their kids to prepare them for adolescence. Keep in mind that you have to mentally prepare your child for what's ahead. And that's really one of the main purposes of talking to her about puberty and sex.

A Matter of Urgency

Parents need to understand the urgency and the importance of talking to their daughter about sex, puberty, and her first period. It is not something that they should delay or take for granted. These days, kids have access to the internet and they can come across information that they might not yet understand. Without guidance from the parents, a young person may get the wrong idea about puberty, relationships, and sex. They might go looking for answers in all the wrong places. Therefore, it is very important that the parents be the first source of information when it comes to these delicate topics.

When is the right time to talk to your daughter about puberty and sex? As a parent, you'll have to be a vigilant observer to know if it is time to have "the talk" with your child. Don't base your decision on age because some children develop early and some late. For instance, a girl can have her first menstruation as early as 8 or 9 and as late as 16 or 17 years old. So use your parent's instinct to pinpoint the right time. Giving "the talk" too early may just confuse your child and giving it too late may not be very effective anymore.

Parents need to be perceptive and alert when it comes to their daughter entering puberty. Ultimately, doing this will be a great help to their child. Don't be in denial just because you want to keep your little princess for as long as possible. One good example is being aware when your daughter already needs a training bra or when her usual clothes have become unsuitable. If your child is a big girl, then she will need clothes and undergarments appropriate for her body type. Many moms and dads become blind to this fact because their daughter is just 7 or 8 years old. They think that their child is still a baby, so how can she need a training bra? However, a young girl with developing breasts or a camel toe may be teased by the other kids. This will be confusing for her if she does not understand the changes happening to her body and how she can cope with it. Moreover, her teachers and other parents may also notice that the girl needs to wear training bras and beat you in telling her about it. A perceptive mom or dad can save their daughter from a potentially scarring experience.

Daughters and Sons

Girls develop differently from boys so parents with sons and daughters should not use the same timeline or the same approach when talking to their kids about puberty and sex. In addition, the changes that boys and girls experience are very different so parents need to prepare separately for "the talk" between a parent and son.

Chapter 2: Tips to Keep "The Talk" Easy and Effective

Don't dread the day that you need to give "the talk" to your daughter. Instead, look forward to it, embrace it, and prepare well for that day. Giving the sex talk to your child is, after all, one of your most important duties as a parent. You are preparing your daughter for adolescence and, ultimately, adulthood. Here are valuable tips that all parents can use as they take on this responsibility.

Tip #1: Keep Lines of Communication Open

Your child should feel that she can talk to you about anything. Create an environment where she will not feel afraid or embarrassed to ask questions. Always make time to talk to her, to ask her about her day, and to let her confide in you. At this stage, young girls may want to talk about their feelings for boys, too, not only about the physical changes happening to their bodies. Be sure to be ready when she opens up about a crush. Don't freak out and give a sermon about her being too young to fall in love. Instead, encourage her to speak up, be understanding, offer her support and most importantly, give the appropriate advice.

Tip #2: Provide Honest Answers

When your daughter does ask you a question about puberty and sex, always give an honest answer. The fact that she came to you means that she trusts you and that she thinks that you will be able to enlighten her. Don't evade her question or worse, give a bogus answer. To help you answer her questions better, first, clarify what exactly it is that she wants to know and from this information, provide the answer that she needs. Second, answer her questions one at a time. This will help you provide the right answers and she will be able to absorb the new information much more effectively. Third, allow her to form her questions. Give her time to talk. Don't form her questions for her and don't jump to conclusions. By doing these three steps, you'll be able to give your daughter the answer she needs.

Tip #3: Refresh Your Knowledge

You wouldn't go to war without a gun, would you? Having the sex talk with your daughter is by no means comparable to going to a war, but it would greatly help if you were prepared and knew what you were talking about. It is highly recommended that you brush up on your biology, anatomy, and physiology. You'll be able to provide more accurate and definite replies to your child's questions if you are clear with the terminology, bodily functions, and processes.

Tip #4: Make It Practical

When giving "the talk" to your child, don't let it resemble an extra biology class. You are not her teacher, you are her parent. So talk to her about menstruation, puberty, and sex on a more personal level. Avoid sounding like you're giving her a science lecture. Give practical information that she can use in her daily life such as keeping extra pads in her bag or school locker, what to do when her pants get stained while she's at school, how to handle menstruation cramps, etc.

Tip #5: Stop, Talk, and Listen

Remember to always allow two-way communication. Speak and listen, listen and speak. Don't just deliver a monologue and tell her to scram. This talk is a very important one, so make sure that you connect with your daughter. Give her the assurance that you are always there to listen and if she ever needs advice, she can go to you anytime.

Tip # 6: Pick the Appropriate Time and Place

The best time to tell your daughter about menstruation is when she is around 8 to 9 years old. If you wait any longer, she might have her first period without knowing about it and that could really freak her out. Remember Carrie. When initiating the talk about her first period, puberty, and sex, it is important that you sit her down for it. Don't start talking to her about menstruation while you're walking down the street, shopping, or worse, in a family gathering! Set a schedule for this talk or pick the right moment to broach the subject but remember to sit her down so that she can absorb what you will tell her.

Make sure that her siblings are not around listening and ready to make fun of her. It is also a bad idea to have this talk in front of her friends, family, and relatives. Your daughter considers her bedroom a safe place and it is best to do the talk here where she will be most comfortable. Also, you can prevent interruptions and distractions.

There are moments between a parent and the child when they are most connected. This is the perfect time to talk to your daughter about her first period.

Finally, comfort your daughter with the knowledge that all girls and boys go through puberty and that she isn't the only one experiencing the physical changes and overwhelming emotions. Perhaps, you can tell her that puberty is comparable to the caterpillar stage that every butterfly has to go through. So this awkward stage in her life will pass and she, too, will become a beautiful, confident woman when the time comes.

Chapter 3: Guidelines for Talking to Your Daughter about Puberty

When talking to your daughter about puberty, keep in mind that your purpose is to prepare her for what's ahead. This is also the time to assure her that the changes she will be experiencing are normal. At this point, your daughter may feel insecure about her appearance. She can suddenly have bigger breasts and more pronounced hips, grow taller, have acne all over her once-clear face, and experience mood swings. To a young person these changes can be scary and confusing. As her parent, it is your role to assure her that all these changes brought on by puberty are okay and are, in fact, normal.

Some of the physical changes that can be expected during puberty:

Girls:

- will likely grow taller

- can start getting acne

- the breasts are developing and will become bigger

- the hips and legs will become more rounded

- pubic hair and armpit hair will start growing

- hair all over the body will become darker and, possibly, thicker

- will start menstruating

- can experience mood changes

Boys:

- pimples and acne can develop

- will go through a growth spurt

- the voice becomes deeper

- the Adam's apple starts to show

- facial hair begins to grow

- pubic hair and armpit hair will start growing

-       the penis and testicles become bigger

-       begin to have wet dreams

-       can experience mood changes

It would help to let your daughter know not only about the changes in girls but also in boys. This will help her in dealing with boys her age and those older than her.

It is important to emphasize that every girl and every boy is unique and development stages in puberty will not be the same for everyone. It can be hard for a young girl to deal with her peers when she's the only one who's started with puberty. Conversely, the effect is the same on a child who hasn't undergone puberty when all his or her friends have started experiencing the changes. Time and time again, remind her that every one of her friends will also undergo puberty and that it is okay to be early or to be late.

Chapter 4: Discussing Her First Period

Technically, a girl becomes a woman when she starts menstruating. Menstruation is the body's signal that the woman is now capable of reproduction. However, we all know that a 9-year-old or a 12-year-old girl is, in all aspects, not ready to be a mother. Equally, teenage boys may be able to father a child now, but they are not yet capable of taking on the responsibilities of a father. This is another compelling reason why parents need to take an active role in educating their children about puberty and sex.

Now that your little princess is at the verge of becoming a woman, you have to be there to prepare her for her first period.

Menarche and Menstruation

A major stage of puberty in girls is the menstruation. Your young daughter may feel anxious about having her first period and the best way to assure her about it is to make her understand the menstrual process. Menarche is the medical term used for a girl's first period. Menarche indicates that all parts of your daughter's reproductive system have matured. Every month, a woman will menstruate. Basically, menstruation means the discharge of blood and tissue.

The Menstrual Cycle

Once every month, an egg is produced by one ovary. This egg travels through the fallopian tubes going to the uterus. During this time, the lining of the uterus becomes thick with extra tissue and blood. When the egg is fertilized by a sperm, it will attach to the uterine wall and will develop into a baby. However, when no fertilization occurs, the egg, extra blood and tissue from the lining of the uterine wall will all come out from the body as menstrual discharge.

This cycle will start from puberty and last until the menopausal stage. During pregnancy, the menstrual cycle stops. The menstrual cycles of women can vary. Some have a 28-day cycle while others will have a 24-day or 35-day cycle. The menstrual cycle is determined by the length of time it takes the ovary to produce an egg.

Some girls will have a regular menstrual cycle while it can be irregular for others. If you have any concerns, be sure to consult with a doctor to learn more about your daughter's menstrual cycle. The doctor can also enlighten you and your child about what is and isn't normal when it comes to menstrual cycles. He or she can recommend dietary changes or supplements to regulate your daughter's monthly period or to minimize discomfort during menstruation.

The Female Reproductive System

Moms and dads out there should not worry too much about this part. You don't need to give a full lecture of all the parts of the reproductive system. All you need to have is a basic knowledge of the major parts of the reproductive system and its functions so that you can explain to your daughter about menstruation and reproduction. Familiarize yourself with the major parts of the female reproductive system – the uterus, fallopian tubes, ovaries, cervix, and the vagina. If you can get a diagram, it will be easier for the child to understand the process of menstruation, sex, and reproduction.

Major Parts of the Reproductive System

- **Ovaries** – Two oval-shaped organs where the eggs are produced.

- **Fallopian Tubes** – Two tubes that serve as passageways of the eggs going from the ovaries to the uterus.

- **Uterus** – This is where the eggs go and become fertilized.

- **Cervix** – A canal from the vagina going to the uterus.

- **Vaginal Opening** – Serves as a path for menstrual discharge, sexual intercourse, and childbirth.

Chapter 5: Explaining the Birds and the Bees (aka Sex)

Talking about sex can be a little uncomfortable for you and your child. However, it is absolutely necessary to do it. Your daughter is at a stage in her life where she has raging hormones and unstable emotions. She may have heard about sex from her peers or from TV and formed ideas based on incomplete information. Without guidance and a little education from her parents, she might not be able to fully grasp the meaning of sex and its consequences.

The dialogue between you and your child should include a discussion on pre-marital sex, an awareness of STDs and teenage pregnancy and her responsibilities in safeguarding against their possibilities.

Explaining Sex to Your Child

Sex is the ultimate expression of love between two people. It is not just about carnal pleasure, but instead, it is the highest form of affection for someone we care for. When talking about sex to your daughter, be sure to share this definition of sex with

33

her. Emphasize that sex is not something that should be taken lightly since its primary function is to procreate and continue the human race. It should be a meaningful act, one that should always be shared with someone we truly care for and who truly cares about us

Pre-Marital Sex

The discussion on whether or not to engage in premarital sex will depend on what is acceptable for you as a parent. Will you let your teenage child engage in it? Or will you prohibit your child from having sex before marriage? Whether you decide to teach her that it is not okay to have sex before marriage or otherwise, be crystal clear with your reasons to support it. If you decide that it is okay to engage in pre-marital sex as long as she is responsible about it, then let her know about that, too. Be clear with her limits and responsibilities. You should also tell her about another option –waiting. Explain to her how waiting for the right person can make the experience so much more special.

Many parents do not wish their teenagers to engage in pre-marital sex for obvious reasons. That said, it is advisable that every parent educate their child about contraceptives. This may be an issue to most parents and teenagers may confuse your discussion on contraceptives as a permit to have sex 'as long as it is safe'. For some, the use of contraceptives clashes with a parent's personal principles, and religion can also be a factor. Nevertheless, a parent can still educate their teens about abstinence and the other natural ways to prevent pregnancy.

STDs and Teenage Pregnancy

It is rather common to hear about young girls as early as 11 years old getting pregnant. More due to a lack of education than the hormones surging in our young at this point in their life, they may not know how to control their emotions and actions. For many middle school kids, to be in a relationship with someone of the opposite sex is accepted as normal. The act of sex may be seen by a young person as the only way to express their "young love". Again, it is up to you to educate your child about waiting and the use of contraceptives, whether natural or artificial. Teach your daughter about responsible sex by telling her the consequences of disregarding it. Acquiring a sexually transmitted disease, as a result of unprotected, irresponsible sex, is as common as teenage pregnancy.

Chapter 6: Being Prepared for Possible Questions

For sure, your daughter will have questions or other concerns. She might even be hesitant to voice them because she is not sure how. Again, reassure her that she can ask you about anything and that you will answer her questions the best way you can. To help you prepare, here are some questions that you should expect.

Common Questions Your Daughter Might Have:

• **Why are my breasts growing? Why are my hips bigger now?**

Puberty stage prepares the body for the next stage in human life – adulthood. Every girl will have bigger breasts and wider hips to prepare for motherhood.

• **Why are my breasts bigger/smaller than the other girls'?**

Every girl's physical development is unique and some will experience breast and hips growth earlier while some will experience physical changes at a later pace. A person's body type, which includes how big the breasts will grow to be, is determined by genes. Like the color of your hair or eyes, this will be different for every girl.

- **How come a girl from my class does not have periods?**

  She may be a late bloomer. She will get her periods soon enough because all girls go through the puberty stages.

- **Why is my classmate taller than me now?**

  Many teenagers go through growth spurts, some sooner than others. Your genes also play a major role in determining how tall you will grow to be.

- **What is masturbation? Is it bad? Can I do it?**

  Masturbation is a natural act to relieve sexual tension. Sexual tension can also be diverted or redirected through other activities like sports or hobbies. Whether masturbation is something you will allow a child to engage in is a personal decision; your beliefs and preferences will factor in. Do teach your child that it is always to be done in private. As with most things, it is unhealthy to get addicted to it.

- **Why do I feel all tingly inside when I see the boy I like?**

The hormones in the body can cause you to feel many things. Teenagers often have infatuations and may experience physical arousal which is a little like being excited for a highly anticipated concert or a favorite meal. It is important to think through before you respond and make decisions, by processing emotions in your brain and not so much your heart or your body.

- **Can I shave my pubic hair?**

Yes. Just like the hair in your head or other body parts, it is okay to cut or shave pubic hair. This means there are no health implications to shaving (your personal preferences or religious beliefs may vary). More emphasis must be given on maintaining proper hygiene and being careful if doing so.

Your child may surprise you with the questions she wants to ask. Don't be ruffled, though. Remember that you, too, were once a teenager. You know how she feels and you have first-hand experience about puberty. If you feel a bit overwhelmed when she takes you by surprise with her questions, just remember how you were at that time in your life. If ever you can't answer a question by the book, give her a reply that is based on your own experiences. She will relate to you better if she knows that you have undergone the very same things that she is going through now.

Conclusion

Parenthood is a gift, and every mom and dad does well to be thankful for the privileges of being a parent. Being a parent to a daughter requires much love and dedication for daughters are, indeed, special. Every time a little girl bids farewell to childhood and says hello to growing up, parents experience both happiness and sadness. It is a bittersweet feeling as their little girl is finally on her way to becoming a young woman.

At this point in your child's life, you need to be a strong pillar, good model, and sound adviser. But most of all, you need to be a parent with consistent, reliable support. Be there for her. Talk to her about puberty and sex in a clear and matter-of-fact manner. Prepare her well for the changes up ahead. It is your duty to make her mentally and emotionally ready.

Finally, always consider your child's feelings when talking to her about puberty and sex. Be considerate when unloading information on her. Remember that children her age may not be ready to handle grown-up information. Be alert for what kind of info your daughter is ready for and what she's not yet prepared to handle. Ask her what topics she would like to know about and what topics make her uncomfortable.

With this book, we hope to have helped you as you take on this major responsibility. Now you can equip your child with invaluable knowledge that will help her go through this stage in her life confidently and happily.

Finally, I'd like to thank you for purchasing this book! If you found it helpful, I'd greatly appreciate it if you'd take a moment to leave a review on Amazon. Thank you!

Made in the USA
San Bernardino, CA
12 August 2016